CW00840913

How to grow p
mushro(

Practical guide for absolute beginners

Easy way to grow your own mushrooms

Frank Luft

Table of Contents

Introduction

Psilocybin is a psychedelic alkaloid of the tryptamine family contained in psilocybin mushroom. This type of mushroom is also called "magic mushroom" or simply "shroom" to some people. Psilocybin is also present in hundreds of species of fungi, including those belonging to genus Psilocybe such as Psilocybe cubensis and Psilocybe semilanceata.

The substance content or the psilocybin, in particular, of magic mushrooms varies and is dependent on species, growth, size, and drying conditions. The potency effect duration as well as the intensity of the hallucinogenic effect of psilocybin mushrooms likewise varies according to its species, dosage, setting, and individual physiology.

Effects of psilocybin can be pleasant and even ecstatic. You can also experience a deep sense of connection with others, with nature, and with your environment. Sometimes you can also experience, confusion and hilarity. For those inexperienced people who take a high dosage of the substance, difficult trips may occur when psychedelic compounds are consumed or when it triggered difficult areas of one's psyche.When taken in low dosage, hallucinatory effects include vision of walls that seem to be alive and breathing, flying colors, and animation of different objects.

With higher dosage, the experience becomes less social and often triggers spiritual experience.

There are a number of people who are unusually sensitive to psilocybin that even smaller doses of 0.25 grams of dried Psilocybe cubensis mushrooms can display effects that are usually associated with the use of medium-high dosage. Tolerance to this substance can also disappear after a few days.

Physical and mental tolerance to psilocybin builds and quickly dissipates. Taking the substance more than 3-4 times in a week can result in diminished effects. To avoid this, frequent users usually keep doses spaced 5-7 days apart.

Every culture is pervaded by fear of mushroom poisoning and there are individuals and cultures where these fungi are looked upon with either fear or hatred. Mycophobic cultures, as they are termed, are perfectly illustrated by the Irish and English people. Conversely, there are societies which had been a part of the long history of those who enjoyed using them.

These are the mycophilic societies which can be found anywhere in Asia and Eastern Europe, specifically among the Polish, Russians, and Italians.

These societies have used mushrooms in their delicacies and have as many as hundred common names to describe the wide range of mushroom varieties.

The use of mushrooms by diverse cultures has proven to be extreme. A banker named R. Gordon Wasson had shown his interest in mushrooms by studying these diverse cultures. Anecdotes relative to the use of mushrooms and other sources of psychedelic substances were noted under the aegis of the Catholic Church when Spanish prosecutors made to totally stamp out the use of Peyote - a spineless cactus with psychoactive alkaloids, specifically mescaline. Pieces of evidence were in support of the idea that the relationship between man and mushrooms went back from ancient times among the ancient Sahara desert dwellers that inhabited this vast domain when it was still covered with a large expanse of vegetation (Samorini, 1989).

Archeological findings were mainly of prehistoric paintings and those currently exhibited in Tassili, Algeria could be the most ancient among ethno mycological findings ever discovered which goes back to the Round Heads period (9000-7,000 years ago).

The center of this style is Tassili, but there are also others to be found at Ennedi (Chad), Tadrart Acacus {Libya), and, to a lesser extent, at Jebel Uweinat (Egypt) (Muzzolini, 1986:173-175).

These paintings depicted images of enormous mythological beings of human or animal form, alongside with small horned and feathered beings in dancing stance. Such images covered the rock shelters in the high plateau of the Sahara.

Among images on display at the Tin-Tazarift rock art site in Tassili were masked figures dressed as dancers and surrounded by geometric designs. These dancers individually carry what appeared to be like a mushroom in their right hand. What appears to be even more surprising on these images were the lines that ran parallel and seemed to be coming out of the mushroom to reach the center of the dancer's head?

One of the most important scenes is currently on display at Tin-Tazarift rock art site in Tassili where one can find a series of masked figures in line along with dancers clad in priest's wardrobe and almost covered with long and lively festoons of various geometrical designs.

Each dancer holds a mushroom-like object in the right hand and even more surprising, two parallel lines come out of this object to reach the central part of the head of the dancer, the area of the roots of the two horns.

This double line could signify an indirect association or non-material fluid passing from the object held in the right hand and the mind. Such depiction somehow coincides with how magic mushrooms were interpreted if we bear in mind the universal mental value induced by hallucinogenic mushrooms, which is often of a mystical and spiritual nature (Dobkin de Rios, 1984:194). It would seem that these images and depictions - in themselves were an ideogram which represents something non-material in ancient art - show the effects that the mushroom has fostered on the human mind.

Chapter 1: Brief History of Psilocybin Mushroom

The discovery of mushroom benefits extended way back during the Stone Age. At that time, only a few people including anthropologists were aware of how influential these mushrooms were in affecting human history. People of ancient Greece, Mesopotamia, and India were likewise very responsive to these fungi and their extreme responses varied from the adulation of those who understand the benefits of mushroom and fear for others.

Several historical records revealed the significance of mushrooms. However, there are historians who believed that magic mushrooms may have Pope Clement VII and Claudius II was poisoned with deadly Amanitas. According to the legend, Buddha dies of eating a mushroom given by a person who believed it was a delicacy.

In ancient verse, mushroom was associated with the phrase, "pig's foot". It has been discovered and used by people in 9000 BC especially in North African indigenous cultures as there were representations of these popular fungi depicted on rock paintings. Statues in the formation of what appeared to be mushroom have been found in Aztec and Mayan Ruins in Central America.

The Aztecs were recorded to have used a substance called *teonanacatl,* meaning "flesh of the gods" that many believed to be what we call today as shroom. The magic mushroom or *shroom* as it is called, along with other psychedelic substance from peyote and morning glory was used to induce a trance and produce visions - a way to communicate with their gods.

Spanish missionaries came to the New World in the 16th century. They mentioned about these psychotropic substances. There were recorded stories of how Spanish persecutors made every effort to totally stamp out the use of these psychedelic substances by the native Indians. They subjected them to cruel tortures - beatings, floggings, and even death if they still persisted. One account stated that a disobedient Indian had his eyes gouged out after three days of continuous torture. Then the self-righteous Spanish priest drove his crucifix into the flesh of the Native American Indian and fed him to starving dogs which finally caused his death.

However, though the long history of magic mushroom is tainted with controversies, some believed that none of this evidence pertaining to its connection with spirituality or holiness is definitive and that people are seeing things they want to believe in these ancient manuscripts, sculptures, and paintings.

Somehow, there is confirmation as to the use of the substance by some indigenous tribes in Central America including the Nauhua, Mazatec, Zapatec, and Mixtec.

Westerners began consuming mushrooms in the late 1950s. R. Gordon Wasson, a mycologist was traveling through Mexico to learn about mushrooms in 1955. As part of his study, he participated in a ritual ceremony conducted by a shaman of the Mazatec tribe using mushrooms. These indigenous people can be found in the Oaxaca region of southern part of Mexico.

Wasson wrote about his findings which were published in 1957. Then an editor came up with an article entitled, "Seeking the Magic Mushroom" and citing Wasson's study and from it, the mushroom was called magic mushrooms though he never used the term in any of his writings.

Albert Hoffman, considered the father of LSD, through the effort of one of Wasson's colleagues, Roger Heim was able to isolate and extract psilocybin and psilocin from the mushrooms that Wasson brought back with him from Mexico. The attention of Timothy Leary, the well-known advocate of psychotropic drugs which includes LSD, was caught by the written article and since then pave way for the magic mushroom to become inextricably tied to the hippie movement in their search for a new form of spirituality.

Except for medical research, the use of psilocybin was banned in 1970 though the actual medical research started only recently after more than 30 years.

Chapter 2: Therapeutic Benefits of Psilocybin

Psilocybin is a potent drug with intense psychoactive effects found in various species of fungi. They are referred to as magic mushrooms and some of them could even be found today in your backyard.

Psilocybin had been recognized throughout the history because of its traditional use since the time of the Australian aborigines up to the Mesoamerican cultures whose descendants are still using it until the present time.

Treatment of Cluster Headaches

Often described as the most painful and disruptive headache, cluster headaches are more intense though they don't really last long. This type of headaches is more painful when it attacks during the night than in daytime, disrupting a person's life when they do.

Even up to the present time, there had been no official publication citing psilocybin as a potential treatment for a cluster headache but numerous anecdotal reports indeed caught the attention of those people in the medical world.

It was in the middle of 2000s when medical professionals take interest on psilocybin and LSD as a potential treatment for cluster headaches when a number of patients reported remission of their condition following subsequent self-medication using the substance. Other tried for psychedelic recreation.

A recent survey disclosed that psilocybin can be more effective in treating cluster headaches than those medications that are currently available with nearly 50 percent of the participants-sufferers vouching for its effectiveness.

From 1960 - 1970, there was a number of pre-clinical trials conducted that had spoken of the promising role of psilocybin and other psychedelics in the treatment of some disorders like cluster headaches, addiction, and mood disorders.

Since its reclassification by the government as schedule 1 drug in 1972, research on the therapeutic effects of psilocybin had been hidden until recently. Numerous anecdotes have caught the interest of those in the medical world along with funding support towards the scientific study of psychedelic mushrooms. Among those who were interested were the Beckley Foundation and MAPS.

Treatment of Moods and Anxiety Disorders

Local stories and anecdotes are pointing to the fact that psilocybin is an effective treatment for mood disorder including anxiety and depression. Dr. James Fadiman had been gathering these anecdotes for years and was surprised with the overwhelmingly positive results. It was only recently when the federal government has allowed minimal and highly controlled studies on psilocybin possible treatment of moods and anxiety disorders. A small pilot study on the effects psilocybin on depression and anxiety on patients with terminal cancer was conducted in 2011.

These patients were in an advanced stage of cancer and clinically diagnosed with stress and anxiety related to their illness. The researchers conducting the study observed significant improvements on measures of depression and anxiety after treating them with psilocybin up to six months after the trial.

When used in a small study of patients who didn't respond to conventional serotonin reuptake inhibitor (SRI) drug medication, psilocybin treatment has successfully reduced symptoms of obsessive-compulsive disorder (OCD) by 23-100 percent.

Treatment of Addiction

When used in a preclinical test to treat addiction in the 50s and 60s, psilocybin showed promising results, but then many of these so-called *cassis hallucinogens* were declared illegal in the United States and in most part of Europe that researches pertaining to its therapeutic value came to a halt. However, recent year once again bring the resurgence of psilocybin and other psychedelics as therapeutic tools in the treatment of addiction.

In a study conducted in 2015, psilocybin, when integrated into an assisted treatment pan has shown potential for treating alcoholism in non-clinical trials. A significant reduction in drinking, as well as abstinence from it, was observed after the administration of psilocybin as part of the treatment program.

Psilocybin substance is likewise found to be effective in helping people to quit smoking. In some trials, 2-3 treatment sessions with 15 participants, the substance as an integral part of a larger cognitive-behavioral therapy program to stop smoking prove to have an 80% success rate in 12 subjects compared to a conventional stop smoking method using patches, gum, cold turkey, etc. which got a 35% success rate.

Chapter 3: Effects of Using Psilocybin

Several studies have associated the psychoactive substance in shroom with several therapeutic benefits including its capability to provide relief from anxiety and depression. However, just like any drugs, it comes with risks and because it is still considered illegal in some countries especially in the US and in some parts of Europe, it's hard to point out what it can do.

Here are some reported ways that shroom can affect your body and brain:

It Brings Relaxation

The National Institute on Drug Abuse compared the effects of using psilocybin mushroom as similar to what one can experience after taking a low dosage of marijuana. Like other hallucinogenic drugs including LSD or peyote, magic mushrooms are said to impact neural highways in the brain that use *serotonin* - a neurotransmitter that can affect mood, appetite, digestion, sleep, memory, social behavior, sexual desire, and functions. To be more particular, psilocybin in magic mushroom can affect the prefrontal cortex of the brain or that part that is responsible for regulating abstract thinking and thoughtful analysis. It also plays a key role in moods and perception.

It Makes you Hallucinates

Users of psilocybin often describe seeing sounds and hearing colors as effects of new links across previously disconnected brain regions.

According to researchers, new stronger activities across several regions of the brain that were rarely or were never previously used were seen in people when injected with 2 milligrams of the psilocybin substance.

David Nutt, a neuroscientist at Imperial College London and author of a 2012 study on psilocybin, also found changes in the brain activity patterns of people on the drug. While there are areas that become more pronounced, others were muted including the part of the brain that is associated with maintaining the sense of self.

While connections between brain circuits in this sense-of-self region are too strong, Nutt further believes that in depressed people, their brains become over connected. But as these connections are loosened and new ones are created, the thinking continues and provides intense relief. Since 1960, there are isolated cases of hallucinogen persisting perception (HPPD) disorder.

Meaning, hallucinations persisted long after one had taken the drug which is typical among LSD users. There are likewise anecdotal reports gathered from people using shroom.

Authorities have yet to come up with the strict and clear definition of HPPD. *Dr. John Halpern,* a psychiatry professor at the Harvard Medical School and lead author of the latest review of HPPD told the New Yorker that based on some other twenty related studies - conducted since 1966, some individuals who have used LSD experienced persistent perceptual abnormalities suggestive of acute intoxication and not attributable to another medical or psychiatric condition.

Helps in the Treatment of Depression and End-of-Life Distress

As disclosed by two studies conducted on patients suffering from depression and distress, a single dose of the psilocybin can be a powerful tool for treating depression and anxiety. The first six months after conducting experiments, 80 percent of the John Hopkins study participants showed significant decreases in symptoms of depression and anxiety based on the gold standard psychiatric evaluation.

The New York University study focused on the effects of the drug substance on cancer patients with severe anxiety. On this study, researchers observed a quick transformation on the insights of participants who received a dose of psilocybin in pill form.

One of the participants, *Nick Fernandez,* says that the experiment took him on an emotional journey that let him see a much greater force than himself! Nick further said that something in him snapped leading him to quickly realize that all his anxieties, insecurities, and defenses were not something to worry about. This result is considered to be a healing process as Jeffrey Guss; a New York University psychotherapist told the New Yorker that many participants experienced the same result.

It is further reported that quite a number of these participants experienced discomfort and intense anxiety for a few minutes or hours. It was only later that they began to feel relieved and experiences vary significantly from one person to another.

Out-of-the-Body Experience

Psilocybin in shroom can induce psychedelic experiences that seem so real.

These type of experiences in which users can see a vision of themselves like in an out-of-body experience can be encountered within 20-90 minutes after taking the drug. It can even last for as long as 12 hours according to the National Institute on Drug Abuse. Experiences can vary depending on the amount of dosage, mood, surroundings, and even your personality.

Slowing Down of Time

While on the drug, your sense of time can be somehow distorted. According to the National Institute on Drug Abuse, a person on this drug feels as though time has been slowed down.

More Open and Imaginative

After experimenting with the drug, participants of the study declared to the group of researchers that they felt they have become more open and imaginative. They also became appreciative of beauty.

Improves Personality

When the researchers followed up with the participants a year later, nearly two-thirds said the experience had been one of the most important aspects of their lives while close to half continued to score high on a personality test of openness than they had before taking the drug

Chapter 4: Myths and Dangers

Myth #1 - Mushroom causes bleeding of the brain, in the stomach, and kidney failure

An internal hemorrhage in the brain is often diagnosed as an aneurysm or stroke. There was no evidence of this ever happening after consuming psilocybin mushroom nor was there any proof suggesting that this magic mushroom caused stomach bleeding.

In 1981 a study revealed that the two most common complications resulting from the use of magic mushrooms were dilated pupils and overly sensitive reflexes. However, other literature reviews claimed they have found no complications of mushroom when used by healthy individuals.

Regarding the kidney problem, species Psilocybe semilanceata where hallucinogenic mushrooms belong have no effect on the kidney. But those belonging to family Cortinarius are often mistaken for Psilocybe semilanceata are harmful to kidneys.

Myth #2 - Magic Mushrooms Can Cause Insanity

Some similarities between "trips" produced by psilocybin mushrooms and psychotic symptoms of schizophrenic individuals have been drawn by researchers, and in almost all cases are proven to be temporary in nature. Even those who were rushed to the emergency room after consuming magic mushroom quickly recovered within hours and get back to their normal mental and physical state. Another study likewise discovered a reduction in the likelihood of psychological distress and suicidal attempts among psychedelic users of LSD, shroom, etc.

Myth # 3 - Magic Mushrooms are Poisonous

Psilocybin is considered as the least toxic of the hallucinogenic substances. Its potential for drug dependence or addiction is minimal and even non-existent. When one uses traditional measures of acute toxicity such as LD 50 or the dosage required killing 50% of experimental animals like guinea pigs). Psilocybin has an LD50 of 280 mg/kg.

To compare, the LD 50's of THC or the active compound in marijuana, LSD, and mescaline are 42 mg/kg, 30 mg/kg, and 370 mg/kg. So when death is the basis for the endpoint of toxicity, psilocybin is not considered toxic.

All these support the contention of the relative safety of psilocybin compared to other narcotics. But injuries and fatalities are resulting from falling or car accidents caused by short-term behavioral and perceptual impairment. In a survey of adolescent Psilocybe users, about 13 percent are reported to have serious injury including loss of consciousness and head trauma.

Chapter 5: Preparation, Materials, and Equipment Needed Mixing Bowl

Large metal or plastic is mixing bowl for mixing substrate. Choose something with the cover so you can easily cover it when necessary.

Mixing Spoon

A long kitchen spoon is for mixing substrate after placing it in the mixing bowl. A metal or plastic spoon is preferable to the wooden spoon.

Measuring Cups

Measuring cups (1/4 cup, 1/3 cup, 1/2 and 1 cup sizes). You will be using them for measuring substrate ingredients.

Organic Brown Rice Flour

The organic brown rice flour serves as food for mushrooms. It needs to be organic so as not to include preservatives. Most rice varieties that are available in supermarkets are loaded with preservatives, so make sure to get this from a reliable source.

Because organic rice carries no preservatives, it is always subject to bacterial attacks when stored. Store it in a well-sealed, light-proof plastic bag or container and always keep it in the dry cool area that is well sanitized.

To make your own rice powder, grind regular organic brown rice powder in a coffee grinder and grind it fine - to the same size as when you grind coffee. Homemade ground brown rice flour is as good as the brown rice flour sold in the market if you use the organic brown rice.

Vermiculite

Vermiculite is spongy volcanic gravel often used in potting soil and sold in different sizes. Choose the large-size vermiculite or the coarse type as it allows the cakes to colonize faster than when it does in smaller or medium-size vermiculite.

To start with, you need a gallon-size bag of vermiculite. It will last for several crops of mushrooms. You can purchase this in any hardware or commercial gardens in your area. Vermiculite is made of amino-silicate clay material mined and processed through heating to expand its particles.

It is sterilized and soaks up to it's 3-4 times the volume of water. It also attracts minerals including calcium, phosphorous, potassium, and magnesium. By itself, vermiculites have no water or minerals but it retains whatever moisture and nutrients are added to the cakes.

Electric Drill or Hammer and Nail

An electric drill is for driving holes in lids of metal jars. You can also have the option to use hammer and nail. The nail or drill bit must be about 2mm in diameter.

Half-Pint-Tapered-Wide-Mouth Canning Jars

The one-pint and half-pint wide-mouth canning jars are common. If possible, choose the half pint-size of about 8 oz or 250 ml. The smaller jars will colonize faster so you can harvest quickly. Though you can use the one-pint jar, you have to double the number of materials to use in the given direction.

Aluminum Foil

Select one that is large enough to make a 6-inch square for each jar. This is available in grocery stores.

Rubbing Alcohol

Choose also the alcohol with 50% or higher isopropyl for sterilization purposes. Buy this from any drug store.

Pressure Cooker

Choose a 4-quart or larger size pressure cooker - the larger the better to use. You can put about 3-6 jars in it depending on the shape of the jars and the pressure cooker. You can sterilize up to 8-12 jars (1/2 pint) at a time. Just make sure that you are aware of the precautionary measures in using it for safety reasons. Seals, valves, and safety plugs should be in working order.

Pressure canners can work with larger volumes of jars. Some even have racks so you will not find it hard to arrange them inside and you can maximize the number of jars to sterilize in one session. However, these types are more expensive than pressure cookers and are unavailable in some areas.

Equipment for Inoculation

Psilocybe Cubensis Spores

At the start, the magic mushroom grower should get a strain of the *Psilocybe cubensis* as it is easy to cultivate. fter acquiring the skill in mushroom growing, you can later try the harder-to-grow types.

Psilocybe cubensis spores are not easy to find in the USA so try to ask someone who grows mushroom where they can purchase this type.

There are several strains of Psilocybe cubensis and here some of the popular ones.

B+

Originally called "Herbens B+ strain", this is the most potent among cubensis. This strain can colonize fast and grows fruits quickly. Fruits are usually large and in abundance making it a suitable choice for first-time growers. It likewise grows in a variety of conditions. Perfect colonization temperatures are 84-86 while it's 74-78 for fruiting.

Cambodian

This strain emerges from Angkor Wat, Cambodia and also considered a fast colonizer with beautiful fruits. It is likewise potent.

Ecuador

Due to its growing ability and stature, this strain has become a favorite of many. It is a good choice for those who just started with the shroom culture because it produces large fruit with nice flushes. This strain is easily identifiable with its meaty stalks and fruits that easily grow on almost any substrate. Colonization temperatures are 84-86 while fruiting is optimal at 74-78. As this species mature fast, picking g must be done in advanced primordial stage right before it breaks its veil if you expect good potency. Like the Hawaiian, Ecuadorian gives out a yellowish glow all over before its veil breaks.

Hawaiian

The Golden Teacher as it is called is a cubensis species with large fruits, especially in later flushes. It is characterized by hard, meaty stalks with dark spots on its cap. When a fruit is cut or bruised, there is an extreme reaction of turning bluish in color. Colonization temperatures are 84-86 degrees while fruiting is 74-78 for optimal.

Tasmanian

This strain displays an excellent fruiting ability. Fruits are large and extend up to 8 inches with caps that are light yellows in color. It also quickly recovers in between flushes.

Acadian Coast

This originates from Louisiana with extremely rhizomorphic mycelium. Fruits are usually medium to large and have a prolific pinset.

PES Amazonian

This type produces fruits in abundance with an average size of six inches and also a fast colonizer. It also performs well in a cool temperature with above average rhizomorphic mycelium.

Hauula

This strain came from the southern part of Mexico in the Oaxaca region. Characterized by long skinny stalks and caps in shapes of cones, its size ranges from 6-10 inches in length.

Plantation Mystery

This is beautiful strain bearing average size fruits with average colonization speed.

Gulf Coast

This Psilocybe strain emerges from the coastal region of Florida and is very potent. It produces average-large fruits in quantity.

Panama

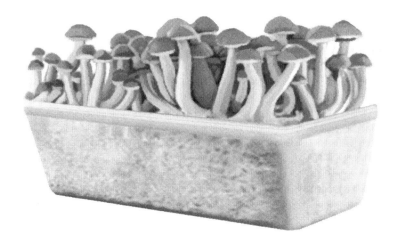

Another fruitful strain of Psilocybe cubensis that is sure to please.

Thailand Koh-Saumi

This cubensis comes from the Isle of Koh-Saumi. Though fruits of this strain are small to medium, they are somehow potent. Has de from being a good colonizer, it is highly resistant to contaminants, therefore, a good one to start with when you intend to grow shroom.

Puerto Rican

Known to have extremely rhizomorphic mycelium, the Puerto Rican is a quick and aggressive colonizer that produces medium to large fruits.

Mazatapec

From deep in Southern Mexico, this hard classic strain is sought after for spirituality reasons. It has great potential of bearing abundant fruits characterized by an aggressive rhizomorphic mycelium.

Treasure Coast

The Treasurer Coast strain is popular for producing albino fruits or lightly caramel in color in some cases. It is also a very fast colonizer.

Argentina

The Argentine species yields massive production of the mushroom of mediocre size and flushes and with continuous flushes. It's known to grow on alder wood and fruit, dung, straw, rice and apparently favored finch or bird seed. It is easy to breed and can thrive indoor breeding. It certainly produces lovely prints.

Mushroom Spores Print vs. Spores Syringe

With a print, you collect sprint on a surface and scrape the spores into sterile water. Then, using a syringe, you suction the spores from the water.

Generally, you can collect more spores from a print than from a syringe. A syringe is taken from a spore solution that is collected from a print. Usually, one can produce 10-100 syringes out of a print.

For sources of spores, you can easily purchase them through online sources. You may use TOR browser for a more extensive search of these online sellers. Take note however of any legality is concerning purchasing and import of the magic mushroom spores depending on your location. This book includes a chapter on its legality, so don't fail to read it up to the last page.

Pair of Dishwashing Gloves

Get yourself a pair of new and unused dishwashing gloves and use them specifically for this purpose. You can get them anywhere in any department or grocery store.

Equipment for Fruiting and Harvesting

Fruiting Chamber

Camping cover, aquariums, and large plastic Rubbermaid storage containers are suitable fruiting chambers. When growing in a low light area for your mushrooms and you need to supply it with an additional source of light, use something with a clear top as a fruiting chamber to accommodate light from outside. When you use dark top chambers, it will not be able to penetrate through it and can't supply the mushroom inside.

Perlite

A silicon-rich volcanic rock, perlite is mined and heated to expand its particles and soak up water. This is used to provide your fruiting chamber with high humidity. Just soak perlite in water, drain in a colander, and place it at the bottom of the fruiting chamber. You may also use vermiculite instead of perlite.

Plastic Colander

A plastic colander is for draining water out of the perlite while being used in the fruiting chamber.

Plastic chambers are best suited to this purpose but suitable substitutes include a piece of cloth or screen that can hold the pirate and yet drain the water off it.

Dust Mask (Optional)

Perlite is puffed volcano glass and when you work on it, it can throw off dust and create a cloud of dust glass which can be harmful to your respiratory system. It can likewise pose a problem in your health especially if you are asthmatic or have a history of respiratory issues. To avoid this, wear a dust mask which you can purchase in a hardware store especially in the paint section. They are affordable and can be helpful to prevent breathing in a germ-filled air over your cakes and terrariums while working with your mushroom project.

Chapter 6: Summary and Procedure - Substrate Preparation

This growing technique is simplified for people who have never experienced before on how to grow magic mushrooms. This is a reliable and proven method to grow magic mushrooms.

If this is the first time to use this method, you need to follow directions exactly and without innovations if possible. Innovations without the experience are the usual causes of failure in mushroom growing particularly when it involved magic mushroom.

However, when you are forced to innovate because you can't find a particular item or for some reasons or another, first check with anyone who is experienced enough to make sure that what you are doing is right and fine.

A Quick Summary of the Procedure

A substrate consisting of a mixture of organic brown rice flour, vermiculite, and water which in a pressure cooker will feed and supply water to the magic mushrooms is sealed in half-pint containers or jars and sterilized in a pressure cooker of boiling water. This is to kill microorganisms that can cause harm to the mushrooms and prevent them from growing.

After the mushroom substrates have been sterilized and cooled, mushroom spores are then added to the substrate with the use of a syringe full of spore solution. The spores will germinate and colonize the entire jar filled with the substrate. These are germinated at about 75-85 degrees Fahrenheit in a dark place. Then remove the produce cake from the jars after they are fully colonized and place in a terrarium with temperatures between 75-80 degrees until (mushrooms) start to grow from the cakes.

After Mushrooms are Formed

Magic mushrooms grow best at 80-90 degrees with 90-95% humidity in a place that gets some light. Once they turned mature, they are harvested and dried. Mushrooms that are grown and produced are 2 to 3 times more potent than those you purchased from other sources. It is because your home-grown magic mushrooms are fresh and have grown under optimal conditions while those from other sources are usually several months old and have grown wild outdoors.

Detailed Substrate Preparation Procedure

Step #1 - Preparing the Jars

Poke holes in the lid of a half pint jar using either a dry or nail and hammer. One hole is enough for a lid but not limited to it. You can have 2-4 depending on your preference. This way they can inoculate the cake in more than one spot. With more holes, you can have the advantage to quick colonization of the cake since growth starts in several places. The disadvantage though is that every time the syringe is inserted into the cake, there is a chance for contamination. So make sure that you wipe the syringe with rubbing alcohol before inoculating every hole.

Most guide resources are suggesting for four holes. When you do this, make sure that the holes aren't too close to the edge of the lid. It must be approximately 3/4 inch or 2 centimeters from the edge of the lid.

Step #2 - Mix up the Substrate

By following the guide we have here in the table below, use the appropriate quantities.

For every jar, thoroughly mix 2/3 cup vermiculite and 1/4 cup water in a mixing bowl and then drain excess water using a disinfected strainer.

Add 1/4 cup of the brown rice flour to the bowl and mix it with the vermiculite mixture. Use a large spoon in mixing it thoroughly.

This will need enough patience and wear out your arms a little. If you are not sure of the sanitation of water in your area, you can use distilled water instead of tap water. But in most cases, water from the faucet is just fine; the recipe provided here often comes out to be a bit more than what you actually need for the jars. Simply discard any excess substrate.

Don't try to pack them in jars because they need to be airy and fluffy for optimal growth.

The Amount of Material for Each Jar

- 2/3 cup (5.25 oz.) Vermiculite
- 1/4 cup (2 oz.) Water
- 1/4 cup (2 oz.) Flour

This mixture is good for 1/2 pint (about 8 oz. or 250 m.) jars. Make an adjustment on the volume of ingredients if you use different size of jars. So if you use one pint instead of half-pint jars, then you need to double the amount of material for each jar.

Step #3 - Add Substrate to the Jars

Using the mixing spoon, fill up the jars with materials up to about 3/4 or 2 cm from the top of the jar. It is crucial that the substrate mixture is open and airy and not packed tightly into the jar.

Dump the mixture in and shake any excess back into the bowl.

Never fill it up to the brim. You still need an open space for the mycelium to grow in. Sterilize the top portion of the jar (the vacant part) with rubbing alcohol.

Step #4 - Seal the Jars

Make sure that you carefully clean the rim and the exposed inner wall of the jar. Fill it to the top with clean dry vermiculite and then cover the lid tightly.

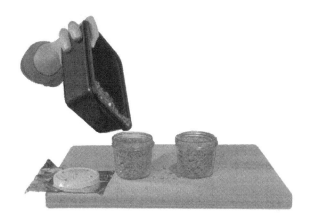

Then cover the lid with a large aluminum foil cut into a square and secure it with a band to prevent water droplets and condensation from getting into the jar.

You can have the option to pace breathable tape like the cloth surgical tape over the holes. This is to ensure that the substrate is insulated from contaminants.

Now your jar is sealed and ready to be sterilized.

Step #5 - Sterilizing the Jars

Line the pressure cooker with a small towel or paper towels and arrange the readied jars on top of it. Make sure that the jars don't tap the base. Add water up to the eve where it reaches half of the jars.

Cook for 40-60 minutes at 15psi following the instructions for your pressure cooker/canner. Leave it to cool completely. Remember not to try opening the pressure cooker while it is still hot and don't try to speed up the cooling process. An abrupt change in temperature can cause the jars to crack.

Be sure to cool the jars for several hours because even when the jars feel cool on the outside, still there is some heat trapped in the center of the cake.

Trying to inoculate too soon after cooking can kill the spores. It's best to leave your jars overnight. The jar containers are not sealed containers of the storage substrate and if you have done everything correctly they can be stored for the indefinite period or until they are needed.

Steam Sterilization

Another way to sterilize your jars is through the steaming process. Any container or pot with tight closing lid and can be able to hold a number of jars are fine. All you need is an environment with a hot temperature that will kill germs in the jar but never add or remove water from the jars you are sterilizing.

Also, try to put something at the bottom of the jar to hold the jars and prevent them from touching the bottom of the pot.

You may use a three-piece vegetable steamer (pot, basket, and lid). You may also opt to use stainless steel vegetable steamers that fold out and stand on the bottom of the pot. If you have no other more convenient choices, then use some rocks or marbles at the bottom of the pot and then place the jars over them. The key point here is for the jars not to touch the bottom of the pot.

Then add enough water to cover about half an inch of the jars. Care should be taken to prevent water to enter the jars once it starts to boil. Using aluminum foil, cover the top of the jars and tighten it with a rubber band. Any extra water will increase the moisture content too much.

Gently steam the jars by boiling for about an hour, keeping the bottom of the pot filled with water by checking the level of water and adding water as the steam evaporates. A good tight fitting lid is vital for successful steaming. Make sure you don't overheat the jars as the substrate will dry out. A gentle and constant boil is suggested. As soon as the inside temperature has dropped below 35 degrees Centigrade or 95 degrees Fahrenheit. To make sure that you'll get 100 percent success rate using this method, sanitation is vital. Sanitize everything including your hands with a rubbing alcohol.

If possible, take a shower before working on a mixing and inoculation materials and equipment. Also, clean the inside and outside of the jars with rubbing alcohol after driving holes on the caps and seeing them.

To make sure that everything that comes in contact with the jar - inside and out is free from any form of contamination, sterilize tables, mixing bowls, tables, etc. using rubbing alcohol. Before adding water to the cake, make sure that it was boiled and leave to cool for a few minutes before using. If you don't have access to a pressure cooker or canner, be extra sterile and you can have 100% can cakes.

Step #6 - Cleanliness Precautions

Inoculating the jar is a major step where contamination is possible to set in and must, therefore, be done in a clean environment.

The needle of the syringe can carry bacteria and spores from other molds that can be transferred to your cake causing it to be contaminated and ruined. Wash your hands and face with antibacterial soap and wear clean clothes. Anything within the contact of your syringe and jars could contaminate your cake when it is not properly clean and sterilized.

Glove Box (Optional)

When you are concerned with cleanliness and sterility, the best way to accomplish this is to make a glove box. A glove box is an enclosed, semi-sealed box with a see-through top and has holes for gloves to go through. You can build one for just a few bucks. To do this, you just need a large cardboard box, some tape, and a saran wrap to go over the top of the box. You will also need a pair of new, unused dishwashing gloves. Tape saran wrap over the top and then cut two holes on the sides big enough for your arms to get through. Disinfect the gloves and the inside of the box.

Oven Inoculation: Cleanliness Simplified

If you have an oven, you can forget all about the glove box. The simplest and easiest way to assure cleanliness during inoculation is to do it on an oven rack.

Turn your oven on at the lowest setting. Once preheated, pull out one of the racks nearest to the edge but not falling out of the oven. Use the one at the bottom. Have your jars and syringe ready. Place 3-4 jars at a time on the edge of the oven rack and carefully incubating them with the syringe.

It's a good idea to have a lighter which you can use to sterilize the needle. To do this, just put the needle over the flame of the lighter until it gets very hot, then carefully squirt it with a little bit of spore solution to cool down the needle before you begin to stick it into the cake. Injecting your cake using a hot needle will only result in burnt rice sticking all over your needle.

Step #7 - Spore Injection

As you prepare your spore syringe and needle, make sure to avoid contamination in the process especially when your syringe and needle require assembly. Using a surgical mask and sterilized latex gloves can help but the safest way to do is to assemble the syringe inside a glove box or where there is still air.

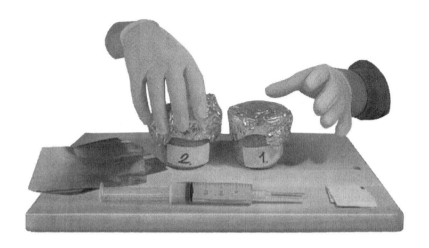

When you are ready to inoculate, simply shake up the spore syringe to get as many spores as you can off the sides of the syringe and into the water.

Carefully remove the cap over the syringe to slide the needle into one of the holes through the jar lid. Shove the needle all the way in until it reaches the cake.

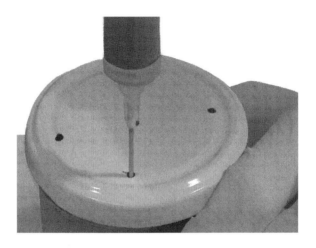

Then gently squeeze out about 0.5 to 1 cc of the spore solution per jar. If you have more than one hole, split the content. However, you may be successful with even just half a cc of each. Make sure that only the jar and substrate touch the needle and recap it right away after using to avoid contaminating the needle. Also be careful of using too much of the spore solution.

With spore syringes, you may accidentally push the plunger of the syringe too forcefully and dump too much of the solution into the cake. Once each jar is inoculated, then it is ready for incubation. Put tape over the holes in the lid to keep out any contaminants.

Keep your jars in a dark place.

Chapter 7: Mycelia (Vegetative) Growth Procedure

Incubation

Now, you have your jars incubated in a dark place at about 75-85 degrees Fahrenheit for several weeks. If you have a room available and constantly kept at this general range of temperature, then it is a good place to have your jars incubated. If none, you will need to find some source of heat to keep your pace of incubation within that temperature range. However, make sure not to use a heat source that could lead to a fire breakout. A heating pad usually works on this while some people use fish tank heaters submerged in a warm water bath.

You can also invest in a thermometer that keeps track of the highest and lowest temperatures so you can see how hot or cold your cake is getting. Once they got too cold it can affect their growth (slow growth), but once it gets too hot, it quickly loses water and eventually wilts. They usually die when the temperature turns 95 degrees Fahrenheit.

Step #8 - Watch for Mycelia Growth

The initial signs of mycelia growth must appear within 5-7 days.

If still, none appear within two-week time, and then it's an indication that something went wrong along the way. Perhaps, it could be that the cake was not cooled completely before inoculating it, and the heat somehow killed the spores or there is great possibility that the spores simply did not make it into the cake.

This type of mushroom mycelium appears to be like brilliant white fuzz, often in ropy strands when growing. This rope-like type of growth is known as rhizomorphic growth and it is an indication that the mycelium will probably grow fruits very well.

Other molds of any color including those less-brilliant white molds - the cobweb mold, for example, is white but not really thick and doesn't even look like cobwebs - are indications of the presence of contamination. A cake that is contaminated will not be able to recover, and except in very few rare cases, will it bears fruits.

Also, watch out for other indicators of contamination including strange smells and colors. As soon as you suspect anything contaminated, get rid of the jars quickly. Dispose it outside in a tightly secured bag and never open the jars or unscrew the lid. If you aren't sure if the jars are contaminated, it always helps to be cautious, so dispose of them even if the substrate looks healthy. There are contaminants that are hazardous to humans.

After 3-4 weeks and you haven't encountered any problem in the process, then your jars have successfully colonized. However, leave it for another week to allow mycelium to hold on more to the substrate. After the colonization is complete, then it's time for fruiting of the magic mushroom.

Chapter 8: Fruiting and Harvesting Procedure

The Fruiting Chamber (Terrarium)

For your fruiting chamber, you can utilize large plastic containers, camping coolers, Rubbermaid containers, aquariums, and other similar things.

Step #9 - Preparing the Fruiting Chamber

The fruiting chamber which is often referred to as the terrarium or growing chamber must at least be 6-8 inches or 15-20 centimeters tall and have enough space for areas for the cake to be arranged with at least I inch or 2 cm of free space on all sides. Spread the cake out as much as possible so that the mushrooms have room to grow. If the chamber proves to be too tall or too large, it might be difficult to keep a high humidity. The bottom of the chamber must be able to contain the required amount of water and the lid must somehow be airtight to maintain needed humidity. It must also be able to shine into the terrarium.

If you are using a cooler or non-transparent plastic container, you will need to cut a window into the top of it and let light pass through and get in, but make sure that humidity can't get out.

For this reason, glass aquarium is indeed a nice fruiting chamber when kept at the right humidity range and temperature.

Inducing Fruiting (Producing Mushrooms)

In order to initiate fruiting, there are three conditions that must be met.

They need dim light as anything warm or bright can harm the cake. Sunlight or light coming from a fluorescent lamp is not suitable. Unlike plants which get their energy from sunlight. For mushrooms, lights send a signal to the mycelium that it's time to produce mushrooms. It's a source with a wide range of colors or spectrum of light, particularly those containing lots of blue light. Examples of light that emits a lot of blue colors are the daylight and fluorescent plant light bulbs. An incandescent light bulb with low wattage (15 watts) will supply enough light.

For fruiting, 90-95 humidity is a good range and the best way to do this is by lining the bottom of the fruiting chamber with damp perlite. A common mistake is for the perlite to be over wet that would end up with a swamp of water. Another mistake is when the perlite is very difficult to clean up and will drown the cakes.

Prepare a one-inch thick layer of perlite on the bottom of the fruiting chamber and place it into a strainer, colander, or any piece of cloth where water can slip out. Wet this thoroughly through a regular tap water and then drain it out. Then transfer the perlite into the fruiting chamber and smooth out the surface. You now have a layer of damp perlite that the cake can be set directly on, and which will keep humidity in the chamber high enough for the cake to fruit.

Once your cake stops producing mushrooms the perlite is expected to start getting a skunk smell. If you intend to reuse it, then put it in a baking pan and let it dries under 350-degree heat in the oven. When it dries up, leave it to cool and it's ready to be used again. You may also add hydrogen peroxide to the wet perlite to help it stay clean.

Make sure that the temperature is about 75-80 degrees Fahrenheit to initiate mushroom growth. Like the light, this temperature range signals the cake to start fruiting.

Step #10 - Birthing the Cakes

Once the white mycelium had completely covered the cake, you can wait up to two more weeks and the cake is ready to be taken out of the jar. When ready, you can transfer the cakes from their jars into the fruiting chamber.

Do this in a very clean room to ensure sanitation. Remove the lid of each jar and then dump out the dry vermiculite on top.

Put the lid back over the top and slowly turn the jar upside down so that the cake is now resting on the lid of the jar. Simply tap the jar gently to loosen up the cake and then remove it from the jar.

Remove the jar from the cake and carefully turn over the cake so it is sitting right side up on the lid of the jar.

Note that it is important that the cake is fruited in the same orientation (same side up) as it was when still in the incubation. If it turned over during the birthing, it will try to grow fruit from the original top side of the cake even when this side is now facing downward. This is not good because mushrooms can't grow properly from the underside of the cake. You will grow very few mushrooms when this happens.

Step # 11 - Dunk the Cakes or Substrates

Taking care not to damage the cakes, rinse each cake under tap water to release any loose vermiculite.

Prepare a large cooking pot and fill it with lukewarm water. Arrange your cakes inside the pot and submerge them in water just beneath the surface using any heavy item like another pot.

Leave them for 24 hours at room temperature for cakes to rehydrate.

Step #12 - Roll the Cakes

After 24 hours, remove the cake from the water and secure them in a disinfected area. Get a mixing bowl and fill it with vermiculite. Let each cake roll over the vermiculite to coat it. This will keep your cakes protected against moisture.

Step #13 - Transfer to Growth Chamber

For each of your cake, cut a square out of a tin foil large enough for your cakes to sit on them.

Spacing evenly, put your cakes in a grow chamber and gently spray mist over the whole chamber using a bottle spray. Before closing, fan with the lid.

Step #14 - Optimize and Monitor Conditions

Mist the chamber by spraying about 4 times in a day to maintain required humidity, but take care not to soak the cake with water.

Fan is with the lid right after spraying about 6 times a day to increase airflow.

Note that some mushroom growers are using fluorescent lights for 12 hours, but during the day, indirect lighting is recommended. Only a little amount of light is needed by a mycelium to locate the open air and determine where to grow mushrooms.

Pinning, Fruiting, and Harvesting

For the first week or two, the colonized cakes generally don't do anything.

Then pins or what others called these very small back-brown bumps, pinheads or primordial will begin to show on the surface of the cake. These are the beginning of the mushroom growth. Many of this spots will never grow large enough but others will grow into full-grown mushrooms. After these formed mushrooms start to grow, the temperature of 80-90 degrees will promote the fastest growth rate.

A mushroom is fully matured and ready to be picked once the edge of the cap separates from the stem. The stem of the mushroom is called the stipe. Often, there is a thin veil between the cap and stipe. If this is present, you can wait until the view is separated before picking the mushroom.

Step #15 - Harvesting Mushrooms

Before sprouting into "pins", fruits or mushrooms will begin to appear like tiny white bumps. You can start harvesting them after 5-12 days.

In picking a mushroom, hold it near the base where is it is attached to the cake and gently twist until it comes off. Immediately after picking it up, start the process of preserving. There are two ways to do it - one is through drying, and another is by refrigerating it.

After the mushrooms were picked out of the cake, you can still have the cake ready to produce more mushrooms by lowering the temperature to the fruiting range of 75-80 degrees.

When you see that new mushrooms start to grow, you can increase the temperature between 80-90 degrees. Each cake will then produce another 1-3 waves or flashes of mushrooms, normally with 2-5 days of dormancy between flushes. After about 2-4 pushes, most cakes are spent and will no longer produce any mushrooms.

Step #16 - Detecting Aborts

Some of the pinheads will start to grow but will suddenly cease growing before they become full-grown mushrooms. We call them as aborts or aborted mushrooms. Aborts are the heaviest mushrooms. A gram of abort will get you more stoned than a gram of fully developed mushroom. Aborts can give you two or three times more stoned than those fully developed magic mushrooms.

However, you need to be quick in picking up abort mushrooms as they are quick to rot. A mushroom that has mold growing on it or which has black goo or slimy substance on the center of the stem is rotten and therefore unsafe to eat.

It is often difficult for beginners to spot an aborted mushroom before it starts to wither.

Warning signs you must watch out for could include a halt in the growth of the mushroom, and the presence of a greenish tinge around the dark-colored tip of the primordial that will eventually turn out to be the cap of the mushroom. Always check and remove aborts from the cake even when they are too rotten for consumption as they can get moldy and cause the cake to get infected.

Chapter 9: Preservation Methods

There are many ways to preserve your magic mushrooms to enhance shelf life.

Step #17 - Preserving your Mushrooms

Refrigeration

If you want to consume your mushrooms right after picking them up, then you can store them in the refrigerator or in a paper bag. Never use a plastic bag to store your mushroom as these can cause them to develop molds. Fresh mushrooms are reportedly more potent than dried ones, but more difficult to dose. Another thing, Cubensis is particularly nasty especially when fresh.

Many people preferred dried mushrooms over fresh ones because drying removes some of the nasty favor. Though most people like the taste of cubensis, yet its taste could vary depending on what strain was used and under what conditions it was grown.

Drying

The best preserving method for mushrooms is to dry them right after you picked them up.

Remember that it is very important when drying for mushrooms not to be exposed to heat. You can have them air dry or dried under the sun, though you can expect some loss of its potency.

Another common method of drying is putting mushrooms in closed containers like a covered bowl that likewise contains desiccant. While drying these mushrooms with desiccant, it will involve long hours, giving more time for the mushrooms to decompose.

You can also dry mushrooms using a food dehydrator. If your dehydrator doesn't include a switch for turning off the heat, then you need to take it apart and disconnect the heating element, making sure to take necessary safety measures. Air-drying so far is the fastest way of drying mushrooms, but will not always remove all of the water from the mushrooms. The drying process can be accelerated by slicing the mushrooms into halves or quarters lengthwise thereby increasing the surface area of each mushroom.

The most effective drying method is to have them air-dried and then to make sure that every bit of moisture in the mushroom was removed, place them into a desiccant chamber.

If you want your mushroom to be brittle and bone dry, make sure that they are not flexible as this will tell you that they are not yet totally dry. Store dried mushrooms in sealed containers and free from heat and light.

By adding some desiccant into the storage container, you can be sure that these mushrooms will stay dry. These little desiccant packets that come in vitamin bottles will work to some extent. You can likewise make your own desiccant packets by wrapping up about a teaspoon of desiccant granules in a paper towel and securing the packet with rubber bands and tape.

Extra Tips

Storing Magic Mushroom

Magic Mushrooms lose their strength as they age and the two worst enemies of the dried mushrooms are heat and light. Always store dried magic mushrooms either in the fridge or freezer and enclosed it in a bag that can't be penetrated by light. A perfect idea is to enclose the mushroom in the airtight bag (Ziploc or the likes). Remove air by squeezing, seal, and put it in a brown paper bag.

Chapter 10: Legality

As to date, there is no record of harm from occasional and sensible use of the substance of psilocybin. On the contrary, there is a growing evidence to suggest that psilocybin and other psychedelics could be used to effectively treat conditions including depression and anxiety. Unluckily, drug policy is based on prejudice and fear and not on reason which is why in most countries, you can be imprisoned for consuming this plant even for health remedies. However, still, there are countries that have more lenient policies when it comes to the use of, purchase, or growing of psilocybin mushrooms.

Countries Where It is Mostly Legal

The following countries have some form of psilocybin completely legal for consumption, possession, and legal to sell and transport.

- Brazil
- The British Virgin Islands
- Jamaica
- Netherlands

Countries Where Psilocybin Is Somewhat Legal

- Austria
- Canada

- Costa Rica
- Czech Republic
- Indonesia
- Mexico
- Portugal
- Spain
- Thailand
- US

As to date, there is no record of harm from occasional and sensible use of the substance of psilocybin. On the contrary, there is a growing evidence to suggest that psilocybin and other psychedelics could be used to effectively treat conditions including depression and anxiety. Unluckily, drug policy is based on prejudice and fear and not on reason which is why in most countries, you can be imprisoned or consuming this plant even for health remedies. However, still, there are countries that have more lenient policies when it comes to the use of, purchase or growing of psilocybin mushrooms.

Countries Where Psilocybin is Completely Prohibited

In these countries, any form of psilocybin is not allowed, so you just can't go out and buy growing kit or spores. You can't possess any of the substance in whatever form and even in small quantities. You are even prohibited to pick up mushrooms growing naturally in the wild.

- Australia
- Bulgaria
- Belgium
- Cyprus
- Denmark
- Estonia
- Finland
- France
- Germany
- Greece
- Hungary
- Ireland
- Italy
- Japan
- Latvia

There are countries that have not approved of the Vienna Convention and thus have no obligation to make psilocybin illegal. They appear to have no specific laws on psilocybin possession and cultivation.

- Equatorial Guinea
- Haiti
- East Timor
- Kiribati

- Nauru
- Liberia
- Solomon Islands
- Tuvalu
- Samoa
- Lithuania
- New Zealand
- Norway
- Poland
- Russia
- South Africa
- Sweden
- Turkey
- Uk

These countries have different laws when it comes to dried or fresh mushrooms and may allow the cultivation of mushrooms or the sale of spores.

Conclusion

Based on different studies that psilocybin can help not only in the relief of anxiety but even in its treatment and prevention is a new hope in this world that's frequently bombarded with stress and anxiety. The result is encouraging but cautions that there is still more work needed before one fully understands how this substance might play a role in combating depression.

As of now, despite the issue of its legality which is locationally bounded, magic mushroom growing had started catching the interests of people who had become aware of its health benefits and hallucinogenic effects.

Through the detailed guidance provided in this little guidebook, beginners can start growing their own magic mushroom in their backyard or anywhere they find it suitable. However, as this could be subject to legality, make sure that you are aware of the regulating laws and policies in your country regarding the growing, use, selling, and transporting of this substance source before starting to grow your magic mushrooms.

F   C
77° 25   In Cupboard

Printed in Great Britain
by Amazon